471 TIMESAVERS
FOR
BUSY PEOPLE

Brian Harris

CGS COMMUNICATIONS INC.
2042 Coral Cres
Burlington ON L7P 3K5 Canada

ISBN 0-929079-26-4

10 9 8 7 6 5 4 3 2 1

INTRODUCTION

We seem to be living at a time when everyone is busy. One of the most common phrases we hear is, "I don't have the time to . . ."

TIMESAVERS FOR BUSY PEOPLE is intended to give you some ideas to help you save time. While it might be expected that this is a book on time management, the author would suggest that saving time isn't a matter of time management as much as it is self-management.

In reading this book, there will be some

suggestions that at first glance appear to be totally unrelated to saving time. Perhaps, after implementing such suggestions into your daily life you will begin to see that saving time includes developing an attitude, a discipline, a focus, and a daily habit of taking responsibility for yourself.

It is recommended that you start by selecting two or three suggestions in this book and implementing these suggestions over a period of a month. Once a few timesavers have become a daily habit, you can then consider trying other ideas given in this book.

1. It is easier to increase your speed when you know exactly where you are going.

2. It takes less time to fix a problem before it happens.

3. Whenever a job seems to be too big, break it down into manageable pieces.

4. When you are listening to another person don't let your eyes wander.

5. When life seems to be passing you by, look for a ramp to take you off the highway.

6. Be careful that yesterday doesn't use up too much of today.

7. Finding a way to become less rigid just might help you to discover the key for solving a problem.

8. Faster is not always better.

9. The best way to build your customer list is one at a time.

10. Whenever possible, avoid travelling on holiday weekends.

11. Small measured changes can make a huge difference.

12. If you use batteries for any electrical device, keep an elastic band on the ones that are new, or fully charged.

13. You may be able to do anything, but not everything.

14. A friend/colleague with a positive attitude is the person you want to spend most of your time with.

15. Working smarter is more important than working longer.

16. In the long run it is less time-consuming to spend some time organizing your desk and drawers than it is to look for papers/materials that you aren't sure where you put them. The same could also be said about your computer files, your briefcase, and even your workshop/kitchen at home.

17. Judging others usually takes up more of your time than accepting them.

18. There may be times when trusting your instincts will be the best and quickest way to get things done.

19. The right answer tomorrow is not necessarily the same answer as yesterday.

20. There is always a cost: understand the demands on your time before you buy.

21. Acceptance of a few moments of solitude can pay interest on your time.

22. Avoid stacking different sizes of plates or dishes on top of each other.

23. Use automatic chequing whenever possible to pay your bills.

24. Concentrate on right now.

25. Spending time enjoying your hobby at home may help you relax at work, even when the two are totally unrelated.

26. A strategy without a commitment is not a strategy.

27. The internet can be a wonderful timesaver, but when you find yourself using it to fill your time like a TV then shut it off.

28. Stand back and observe.

29. The first step in achieving any goal is to write it down.

30. If you are going in the wrong direction, going faster still won't help you.

31. A hot bath or shower can slow down your internal clock when it is rushing too fast.

32. Technology only saves time when you resist being seduced by the technology.

33. When you're really not sure, sleep on it.

34. Only work out of your home if you are the most disciplined person you know.

35. Always do the right thing.

36. Sometimes five 10 minute meetings can be more productive than one 50 minute meeting.

37. Simplicity increases speed.

38. Teach your family to empty their pockets before their clothes are put in the wash.

39. After you finish a task congratulate yourself and take a pause before you begin your next project.

40. Don't shop during peak times.

41. Sometimes in order to do things differently you need to create a new set of tools.

42. If you plan on saving an article from a magazine/newspaper write the page number and title on the front cover so you don't have to waste time trying to find it again.

43. Sometimes we need to live by island-time instead of internet-time.

44. Use two dust cloths, holding one in each hand.

45. Have an exit strategy anytime you are in a situation which has the potential to drag on.

46. The most flexible trees survive the greatest storms.

47. Unless you have a better way of doing it, don't criticize the suggestion you have been given.

48. If it has to be done, then do it.

49. When everyone on the team feels important the team is more efficient.

50. Sometimes it is the attention to the smallest detail that makes the biggest difference.

51. Being positive is less time-consuming than being negative.

52. Just as a small river can carve a path through the mightiest of rocks, change can erode you unless you learn to flow with the river.

53. Identify someone who is successful in the way that you want to be successful and then imitate whatever they do.

54. In completing any task the single most important word to remember is "ACTION".

55. Buy only washable markers and crayons for children.

56. Empower others around you.

57. Give your customers the best experience possible.

58. If you do not like the way you managed yourself yesterday, then change your approach for today.

59. Wash floors and walls with two pails: one for soap and the other for your rinse.

60. As the tides ebb and flow each day be sensitive to the rhythms of the natural world.

61. Stay in control.

62. Sometimes the more timesaving devices that you have results in having less time.

63. When it is difficult to find the time to cook a nutritious dinner every night, spend one night cooking for the week.

64. Before you repair something yourself, ask yourself if the time (and possible aggravation) involved is worth the money saved.

65. Stay calm before you panic.

66. Don't shop for food when you are hungry.

67. Focus on what is important.

68. Use a quality brush when painting.

69. It generally works better to overestimate how much time you need to complete a project than underestimate it.

70. Cut your losses before they become full-blown problems.

71. Basic survival favours those who are flexible and can adapt.

72. Don't work during your breaks or lunch, and especially not during breakfast or dinner at home.

73. At least once a week do something that you think you can't, however unimportant this act may appear to be to you.

74. Learn to filter out the things that just aren't important.

75. A well-coached team will consistently move the ball up the field faster than one individual always trying to do it alone.

76. Ask someone for help.

77. As you work on a project, every once in a while close your eyes and visualize what your final result will look like.

78. If your family doesn't even know that you have a cell phone they are indeed fortunate.

79. Preparation is the master timesaver.

80. You will never see things differently unless you try another pair of glasses.

81. At the beginning of every day identify what you want to accomplish during the day.

82. Politeness in a meeting doesn't necessarily encourage the desired result.

83. Once a year list all birthdays, anniversaries, etc., on a master calendar.

84. The pace at which you start your day generally stays with you throughout the day.

85. A long attention span enhances creativity.

86. Learn to look at your own mind with detachment.

87. If you travel frequently keep a duplicate set of essentials (i.e. toiletry, underwear, socks, extra batteries, etc.) in your suitcase, or in a drawer, ready to go.

88. Instead of burning time, cultivate it.

89. Clothespins can be used to reseal food packages.

90. Practice is integral to success provided that you are practicing correctly.

91. Just as you wouldn't drive your car into a restaurant, don't bring the restaurant into your car.

92. If you need silence to complete a task, then shut the door and take your phone off the hook.

93. It takes less time to buy groceries for the next two weeks in one shopping trip than it does to visit the grocery store every day for a few items.

94. File cancelled cheques, receipts, manuals, guarantees, etc., in a place where you know exactly where they are.

95. If you learn best by example, then spend some time attempting to identify the example you want to learn by.

96. Pace yourself.

97. What you eat often reflects your level of self-discipline.

98. Laugh.

99. Sometimes you need to disconnect every technological device in your life, and other times you simply need to disconnect yourself.

100. Generally, it takes less time to do a job today then it does to postpone it until tomorrow.

101. Allow yourself to experience your feelings.

102. If you need more storage space, what you may really need is a garage sale.

103. When you have to carry some little things wear clothing with pockets.

104. Always be early.

105. Clean a stain from the outside in.

106. Do it right the first time.

107. If you don't have the time to experience it now, then eternity will be too late.

108. Purchase the best vacuum you can afford.

109. Let the web work for you.

110. Consider the potential positive and negative consequences of any action before you take it.

111. Stop whatever you're doing, close your eyes, and concentrate on breathing slowly.

112. Avoid "ifs" and "buts".

113. Knowing who is in charge helps everyone to go faster.

114. If you spend a lot of time sitting at work, a comfortable chair may be one of the best investments you can make.

115. Try using a toilet plunger to unplug a sink drain.

116. Each step in working towards a long term goal should be achievable with a solid effort.

117. Keep a master shopping list in an accessible place in your kitchen.

118. At home, set aside a specific time each week to deal with mail, bills, etc.

119. If you don't like what you see in the future, then create your own.

120. When you are going on a trip with a young child, plan on leaving one hour before your child's normal nap time which should allow you to travel in peace when your child falls asleep.

121. Think big, but start small.

122. It is faster to wash a wall than re-paint it.

123. When in doubt concentrate on visualizing the end result you want to achieve.

124. Inflexible goals are often best achieved by a flexible process.

125. Never use two words when one will do.

126. For many people, time management at home may need more attention than time management at work.

127. Sometimes you need to surrender in order to win.

128. Your mind is either your best friend, or your worst enemy.

129. If light speed is the norm in your work environment, it doesn't have to be the norm in your home environment.

130. Working late on a regular basis usually puts you further behind tomorrow.

131. With clearly defined steps as a part of a major project you can always achieve a sense of completion many times before the entire project is completed.

132. Photocopy, photograph, or video all your important personal records and place the results in a safety deposit box.

133. Learn to excuse yourself from a telephone call that is interfering with what you really want to be doing.

134. Eat a slow, nutritious breakfast.

135. It is faster to copy than to invent.

136. You don't always have to have the right answer, or for that matter any answer at all.

137. Use an oven liner or a piece of foil when cooking meals that might make a mess in your oven.

138. If you feel worn out from constantly handling emotional crises for colleagues/ friends then you should write down the names of some respected community counsellors and refer your colleagues/ friends to these professionals.

139. Being punctual saves time.

140. If you travel often as a part of your job, avoid checking any luggage if possible.

141. If the things that you really want to do don't seem to happen very often then they should become a regular scheduled part of your day.

142. Whatever has been nagging you, get it done immediately.

143. Both winning and losing are habits: which one you live with is your choice.

144. Have a centralized message centre in your house.

145. When you need a quick weather report look out the window.

146. Financial worries will quickly eat up your time. Don't spend what you don't have.

147. There are times when you can do more by doing nothing.

148. People adapt, but the process is easier if you don't allow yourself to get in the way.

149. Avoid formal meetings whenever possible.

150. Return your telephone calls when it is convenient for you.

151. Cancel the magazine subscriptions that you never seem to find the time to read.

152. Respecting the time of others will help them to respect yours.

153. Keep your focus unnervingly on what it is that you want.

154. Goals must be appropriate.

155. It is hard to be interrupted if others can't find you.

156. Learn to ignore your negative thoughts in the same way you might ignore someone who is pestering you.

157. When you have a lot of mail sort it out over a recycling box.

158. If your life would be significantly better if you didn't have to commute so far, what would you have to do to eliminate the commuting?

159. Reduce the time that you watch TV.

160. The main job is always to keep the main job the main job.

161. If you are dealing with a complex problem with a short timeline, the ability of your team to work together may be more important than the speed of your computers.

162. Organize your kitchen, workshop, or office, so the things you use the most are the most convenient to locate.

163. Keep a bookcase near one of your doors and assign each of your children a space. Use it for gloves, scarves, books, notes for school, etc.

164. Use different coloured file folders to represent each month of the year.

165. Minimize unscheduled time.

166. If you know that you are going to be stuck in traffic make sure you have your favourite cassette or CD, whether it is music or educational.

167. Place a paper towel in the bottom of any container you use to hold pens.

168. If a cell phone is an integral part of your daily life, then subscribe to an answering service so you don't feel compelled to answer it every time it rings.

169. Always sit down when you eat.

170. When your children are old enough to safely use a washing machine, teach them how to use it.

171. Pack things away in a manner that makes it easiest to unpack them for use.

172. Dress appropriately for the work you are doing.

173. Learn to delegate.

174. Only put the garbage out the night before if you are sure there are no cats or raccoons in your neighborhood.

175. Sometimes you will be at your creative best when you are doing nothing.

176. Buy quality.

177. If you don't understand how to live in the present, watch a child playing.

178. If you never have a moment for yourself, maybe it's time to ask yourself what you fear about the moment.

179. Taking a sick day before an illness really hits you is better than trying to continue working through the first symptoms and then missing a week.

180. When you are forced to take a detour, always watch for new opportunities.

181. Make your bed and wash your breakfast dishes before you go to work.

182. Keep an umbrella in the trunk of your car.

183. If there is something to learn from criticism, then learn it but don't dwell on it.

184. Keep $20 in a secret place at home and work for emergencies.

185. You can't please everyone all the time.

186. What you think you have to do is often more tiring than what you actually have to do.

187. Valued employees are better workers.

188. Implementing the smallest suggestion might just leave the door open for a big idea that makes a significant difference.

189. Forgive yourself, and move on.

190. There may be times when a task 80% completed today might be better than 100% completed tomorrow.

191. Develop the habit of praising yourself even when others don't.

192. The time is now.

193. Whenever you strike out consider this feedback to improve your swing for the next time you go up to bat.

194. Understanding takes less time than confronting.

195. The best person to sell to is the one who makes the purchasing decisions.

196. Before you leave for any meeting ensure that you have all related materials with you.

197. Keep a schedule of everything you do in 10 minute intervals for a month. After one month look at your results and consider timewasters that you can eliminate.

198. When you have time for only one aspect of housework, then vacuum.

199. When you are driving avoid using your cell phone.

200. Busywork is often the great obstacle to really making significant accomplishments.

201. Two people can generally handle most tasks faster than one person.

202. Your greatest amount of time should be spent on your most important goals.

203. You will never know if you don't try.

204. You can't hit a bullseye if you can't see the target.

205. Be decisive.

206. Wash your windows on overcast days. It is easier to see the dirt.

207. It's okay to be happy.

208. When you have a stain on some clothing, or a loose button, never put it back in your closet until you have it cleaned or repaired.

209. Sometimes when you take a step away from the picture, it looks different.

210. Spending time to take a puppy to obedience school will pay time dividends later.

211. It is easier to manage your time when you feel good about what you are doing.

212. Practise your self-discipline.

213. It takes less time to clean a razor than it does to shave with a dirty one.

214. Unclear objectives waste time.

215. Talk to the person who is most likely to make things happen for you.

216. Learn what habits you have to continually practise to increase your own "good luck".

217. Sometimes by relaxing your mind from trying too hard, you may unleash your natural ability from within to solve the problem.

218. Make it as easy as possible for customers to order products.

219. In every setback look for a new opportunity.

220. A good physical workout can unclutter you mind.

221. Turn if off and come back again in 30 minutes.

222. Have a meeting where laptops and cell phones are forbidden.

223. Doing it the way you've always done it may no longer be the right way to do it.

224. Be a member of an automobile club that offers 24 hour service.

225. When using glue, remember that less is more.

226. Long hours don't necessarily mean you are being more productive than anyone else.

227. Have a written list of tasks you have to complete each day and review the list often.

228. Have a specific place to always put those "little things" like your keys, wallet/purse, etc.

229. Less is generally more.

230. It is easier to extinguish the flame from a match than from a forest fire.

231. Remember that a strong finish is as important as a good start.

232. If your desk is generally covered with small notes to yourself, try keeping one master "TO DO" list instead.

233. When you find yourself asking the question, "When should I do it?", the best answer is usually, "Now".

234. Set realistic deadlines and keep them.

235. Always write your ideas down before you can forget them.

236. Keep eliminating what doesn't work until you find what does.

237. Simplify. Simplify. Simplify.

238. If you are thinking of doing some house renovations attend workshops on related topics at your local building supply store.

239. Stop to talk to someone that you've never talked to before.

240. Sometimes the most obvious answer is neither the right one, or the best one.

241. Don't give away something that isn't yours.

242. Knowing the needs of your customer will save you more time than if you attempt to sell your needs to them.

243. The first step is always just that.

244. Obstacles often occur in proportion to the number of times you take your eyes off your goals.

245. Do something totally unrelated to your work.

246. Use the same time management techniques that are successful at work when it comes to doing household chores.

247. Buy bulk foods whenever possible.

248. If you have to eat fast food, then eat it slowly.

249. Place time limits on any task that you are working on.

250. If the rest of creation enjoys a period of rest every day why should you be any different?

251. If you want to cut back on the amount you travel don't always be every place you have to be in person.

252. Seek a small win every day.

253. To go beyond where you are now may require a different way of thinking.

254. If you require a different answer then ask a different question.

255. Have a strategy when you shop so you don't become distracted into spending time and money on things that you don't really need.

256. A few minutes at the end of each day organizing yourself for tomorrow will usually take less time than if you save the same task for the morning.

257. Take one minute mental vacations.

258. Don't always feel you have to do everything yourself.

259. Always keep some glue and tape in a place where you know they are.

260. If you travel frequently keep a list of the necessities you take on each trip.

261. Solve your own problems before you try to rescue everyone else.

262. If you have the same problem today as you had last week, perhaps it's time to find a new approach for solving it.

263. Action is less time-consuming than reaction.

264. Don't be an errand boy when it can be faxed, e-mailed, or sent by courier.

265. Understand any problem completely before attempting to find a solution.

266. If using a computer is a routine part of your life, a significant timesaver might be to take a course to improve the speed at which you type.

267. If interruptions are bothering you, use your voice mail to monitor your calls.

268. Let others talk more than you.

269. Always be prepared for voice mail when you call by leaving a detailed enthusiastic message that commands action.

270. Don't say "yes" when you really mean "no".

271. If you are constantly disillusioned by not meeting your own expectations, then consider lowering your expectations.

272. Be willing to take some chances on everything, except your reputation.

273. Strive to be more in control of yourself and less in control of others.

274. If you have trouble writing letters, choose smaller stationery.

275. If you have to re-pot a plant in the house then do it in a cardboard box to contain any possible mess.

276. Deadlines are usually less threatening after you have taken the first step in reaching them.

277. Avoid buying a family pet simply because you're caught up in the spirit of a special occasion.

278. Eliminate distractions.

279. Don't be so busy looking at a door that has closed on you that you fail to see the one that is now opening.

280. Whatever paper/magazines you can't handle that are not time dated, place in a box and once a month make a decision on what to do with each piece of material in this "procrastination pile".

281. When painting a room use drop cloths and masking tape to eliminate messy splatters.

282. Know when to remain silent, and practise the skill until you learn it well.

283. If time is money, time with your family will make you very rich.

284. Treat everyone in the workplace as an equal.

285. A positive thinker generally seems to have more time.

286. Use masking tape on the edge of wood that you are sawing to keep it from splintering.

287. Set aside a specific time(s) each day to send/reply to messages.

288. Asking questions saves time in the long run.

289. If you are travelling any distance to a meeting then confirm the meeting before you leave.

290. Most meetings run faster and are more productive with set agendas and time limits.

291. Focus on one task at a time, breaking it down into manageable steps.

292. A happy home is your best friend.

293. Entering appointments, tasks, etc. into a computer based "organizer" program is only a timesaver if you can type the words faster than you can write them on a sheet of paper in a daily organizer (or, in the long run, if the software provides a search, or locator function, that will help you to find things quicker).

294. Schedule some time for yourself with the same promptness and commitment you might make if you were meeting with the president of your company.

295. A satisfied customer makes less time demands on you than a dissatisfied customer.

296. Don't feed your little problems.

297. Pay someone else to do it for you.

298. When you're working ask yourself if what you are doing at the moment is getting you closer to what has to be done by tomorrow.

299. Keep a handy list of the hours of local stores, banks, libraries, etc.

300. There is a rhythm to all living things. Take time to let it speak to you.

301. A great final project is often the result of many drafts along the way.

302. Always keep a pen, paper and a flashlight in the glovebox of your car.

303. Take a one minute physical break.

304. By leaving to and from work at different times, or by changing the route you take, you may save yourself some time.

305. Your ability to enjoy doing absolutely nothing may have a positive affect on your ability to do something.

306. Always attempt to understand before you react.

307. Always, always, back up every piece of work that you do on a computer.

308. Of all the terrible things that you think might happen, only a few may ever really occur, and sometimes none of them.

309. Patience encourages perspective.

310. Always keep sight of the bigger picture while being content with smaller achievements.

311. You will generally be more productive if you keep your schedule somewhere else than in your head.

312. Decide the night before what you will wear for work the next day. If you make your lunch, make it the night before as well.

313. When you face a huge problem find some part of it that you can take control of.

314. Let your conscious mind focus on your immediate work while your sub-conscious mind works on what you have to do tomorrow.

315. Even the best laid plans can meet obstacles. Always be ready to be flexible.

316. Flowers last longer if they are picked in the early morning, or late evening.

317. Always put a date on anything that crosses your desk.

318. Keep a small box of baby wipes handy when you travel.

319. Use different coloured pens on your family calendar to keep track of everyone.

320. When you continue doing the same thing every day for a month you are on your way to developing a habit.

321. You can often remove a sticky substance, such as gum, from your clothing with an ice-cube.

322. If you are constantly driving here and there to save a few pennies you may be stressing yourself more than the few pennies are worth.

323. Check possible roofing problems with a pair of binoculars to save you having to go up on the roof.

324. A vacation is not a vacation if you fill it with the same intensity as your work schedule.

325. Learn to say "NO" with conviction.

326. Arriving at work 15 minutes earlier than you are expected may alter your sense of time during the day in a positive manner.

327. Unless you carefully examine how you spend every minute of every day, it is difficult to organize your time more meaningfully.

328. Sometimes contemplation is better than action.

329. Graphite from a lead pencil can help you with a sticky zipper.

330. To prevent a nail from splitting the wood, blunt the pointed tip of the nail with a light tap of the hammer.

331. Trim the excess.

332. Regular car maintenance not only saves you time, but money.

333. Don't answer your family telephone when your family is eating.

334. If your meetings have a way of becoming too long, try a "stand up" meeting instead.

335. Lighten up yourself and you will lighten up your load.

336. You don't have to catch every ball that is thrown in your direction.

337. In that final moment when your life passes before you what do you want it to look like?

338. If a task in your daily planner is not completed today, move it to tomorrow. Don't spend time flipping pages to find past jobs that you didn't finish.

339. Storage containers that are easily moved will give you greater flexibility than permanent shelving.

340. If you find yourself looking for the same thing today that you lost yesterday, then organize yourself in a way that you will never lose it again.

341. Accurate data entry today results in data integrity for tomorrow.

342. When you're overwhelmed go for a walk.

343. Use a good quality squeegee when cleaning your windows.

344. It is generally best to start your most difficult tasks first.

345. If using a computer is a routine part of your daily life attend workshops to learn the shortcuts/tips associated with the programs that you use.

346. A smile usually saves time.

347. Keep a master list of everything you have to do. Use some system to prioritize which items are the most important to do today. As you complete each item cross it off with a bold stroke.

348. When shopping for a specific single item, telephone the store first to ensure it is in stock before you leave the house.

349. Book your family members back-to-back when you have to visit the dentist.

350. Read the labels on new clothes for instructions on washing before you wash them.

351. It takes less time to do it right than to do it over.

352. Regular maintenance is less time-consuming than fixing something after it is broken.

353. An unrealistic goal generally results in a realistic failure.

354. Ask an expert.

355. Nothing would ever get done if you had to first overcome every possible obstacle.

356. If you can't shake a mop or broom outdoors then shake it inside a plastic garbage bag.

357. Be specific when you are planning.

358. Learn the multi-faceted uses of products like baking soda.

359. Keep your words and thoughts consistent with what you want to achieve.

360. Cooperation may be the greatest asset for the survival of any organization.

361. If you are getting tired of changing washers then install a washerless tap.

362. The key to successful time management is to concentrate on self-management.

363. The smallest step forward brings you closer to your goal.

364. Keep changing your actions until you get the desired response.

365. If you are not sure what to do then find someone who does, and copy whatever this person does.

366. A damp cloth can pick up pet hairs.

367. A good doormat may help save cleaning time.

368. Letting someone else make decisions for you generally costs you time.

369. The only appropriate excuse is that there are no excuses.

370. Goals should always be clearly defined, written down, measurable, and read several times each day.

371. Lack of direction is often the real reason for lack of time.

372. Limits are what you accept in your mind.

373. Interruptions are only interruptions when you give them permission to be just that.

374. Never redo a chore that a child has done for you if you would like that child to do more chores for you in the future.

375. Shopping by yourself is quicker.

376. Encourage people on your team to talk aloud when they are thinking about ways to solve a problem.

377. Know what irritates you and practise strategies for dealing with them.

378. Take a vacation where no-one knows where you are.

379. Before you begin any project arrange all the required materials in front of you.

380. Manuals, or maps, are only useful when they are opened.

381. Sometimes in order to go faster you have to first slow down.

382. Use a pocket comb to hold small nails when hammering them.

383. When you are painting a complete room start with the ceiling.

384. When giving instructions to children ask them to repeat them back to you to ensure understanding has occurred.

385. Being busy and being productive are not necessarily the same thing.

386. It is easier to maintain the speed of a moving object once it is actually moving.

387. Consider all the possible solutions for any problem before you take action.

388. An Olympic gold-medalist often takes a lifetime to prepare for one race.

389. Use different colours to represent different tasks on your daily calendar.

390. The follow-through swing of the bat hitting a home run is as important as the initial explosive start of the bat.

391. When you have to remember to bring something to work tomorrow put it by the door before you go to bed.

392. Pruning is a necessary part of growing.

393. You will move faster when you are concise.

394. Shut off your computer and on a piece of scrap paper outline what you want to do.

395. When planting a tree always visualize how it will look when it reaches maturity in relationship to your house and other parts of your garden.

396. If you knew what you would be doing in 5 years, how would that affect what you are doing today?

397. Before you begin any task always understand what it is that you are really trying to do.

398. There are times when it is necessary to move on to the next question even when you haven't finished the question before it.

399. Why own a big expensive house if you are never home because you always have to work to pay for it?

400. Keep extra pieces of sandpaper on a clipboard in your workshop.

401. Change is a basic function of being alive.

402. Regardless of what kind of day you have had, the sun will still set, so why not enjoy the sunset?

403. What you are doing at any moment determines whether you will have enough time.

404. Waking fifteen minutes earlier than you have to can help you start your day with a more relaxed attitude.

405. Use a pencil in an address book.

406. Stay home for your vacation, but tell everyone else that you have gone away.

407. Latex paint is the easiest to clean up after using it.

408. Start with the uncomfortable work you have to do.

409. Sometimes it is useful to ask yourself how you will feel about the problem that is upsetting you now, a year from now.

410. Try public transportation or car pooling for a few weeks to see what advantages either might have for you.

411. Prioritize all the tasks you need to do and then start with the highest priority first.

412. Keeping a monthly, or even an annual calendar, can help you see at a glance what is coming so there are no last-minute surprises.

413. Paraphrasing what others say to you ensures that you understand them.

414. Read the instructions before you try to put it together.

415. Complete the little things you have to do with the same devotion as the big things.

416. Understand who the people are who are most important to you and spend most of your time with them.

417. It is easier to travel faster in calm waters.

418. Take three deep breaths before you react.

419. Instead of thinking about what you have to do next, focus on what you are doing right now.

420. The best way to ensure a relaxing lunch is to begin by complimenting the person opposite you.

421. If you miss heaven now, you will have trouble finding it later.

422. Positive first impressions save time.

423. It is important to understand whether you are running in a 100 metre sprint, or a 42 km marathon, and then run accordingly.

424. You can dry a few items faster if you add a few clean dry towels of a comparable colour.

425. If you need to be more relaxed and in control, then you have to picture yourself as being relaxed and in control.

426. Whenever you use a tool always put it back in the exact spot you found it when you're finished.

427. Generally, the same old ways achieve the same old results.

428. Comfortable shoes for work might make a difference in how you feel.

429. Avoid people who place unnecessary demands on your time.

430. Be a positive talker.

431. When you find yourself running out of ideas, stop working and stare at an object outside, letting your imagination play with the object.

432. A shortcut is not necessarily the fastest route.

433. Before committing yourself to getting more, ask yourself if you might be happier with less.

434. Keep the phone numbers of your children's friends in a handy place.

435. The path of least resistance often results in more failures than successes.

436. Give yourself permission to do something just for you.

437. A daily planner only becomes a timesaving technique if you use it religiously.

438. Schedule your most important tasks for the time of the day when you know you are the most productive.

439. Learn how to use a "spell checker" on your computer, and if your software program has an automatic spell checker keep it turned on.

440. The speed at which you read for understanding may directly affect the time you spend on a task. If reading is an integral part of your job, and you know your reading ability is slow, then consider taking a course to improve your reading speed.

441. You can prevent long-sleeved shirts from getting tangled in a washing machine by buttoning the sleeves to the front button holes.

442. The purpose of a coffee break is to relax.

443. The more you say "no", the easier it gets.

444. Avoid beginning sentences with "Some day I will …"

445. Before you make any major purchase, research the product carefully.

446. Use horizontal strokes on the outside of a window and vertical on the inside when you wash it. That way, when you are finished, it is easier to know if a streak is on the inside, or outside.

447. Take the time to feel the pain when it confronts you.

448. Pauses are an important aspect of the overall beauty of a music composition. Let pauses contribute to the beauty of your life.

449. Happiness comes from understanding and following your purpose.

450. There are occasions when a picture of a sundial instead of a digital watch may give you a healthier attitude towards time.

451. It is important to have a consistent and quick way of filing every piece of paper that comes your way.

452. Be content throughout every day.

453. Appreciating and thanking others takes less time than criticizing them.

454. Our mind adjusts the scale in the direction that we tell it to.

455. Always keep your dryer's exhaust hose and lint screen clean.

456. Spending too much time listening to negative people may cost you more than just wasted time.

457. Remember that as you plan for tomorrow you can only live in today.

458. Let others finish what they have to say before you respond.

459. Those few minutes in the morning as you wake up may be some of your most precious moments of the day. Fill them with positive thoughts.

460. Even the largest mountain can be scaled one step at a time.

461. Verifying the small details of anything you have to do can be a big timesaver.

462. When your car no longer fits in the garage this is a good sign for you to donate some items to a local charity.

463. New words can encourage new results.

464. You don't always have to see immediate results for progress to be occurring.

465. Wanting to do something needs to be replaced by actually doing it.

466. It is easier to increase your speed when you are not second-guessing yourself.

467. Any moment can be an eternity if you hold it with patience.

468. Long term goals should have a step you can work on every day.

469. When you value your time, other people will value it too.

470. Marketing your successes takes less time than defending your shortcomings.

471. Sometimes, it is the things we didn't think we had the time to do that we end up regretting the most.